All rights reserved. No part of this publication may be reproduced, distributed, or transmitted in any form or by any means, including photocopying, recording, or other electronic or mechanical methods, without the prior written permission of the publisher, except in the case of brief quotations embodied in critical reviews and certain other noncommercial uses permitted by copyright law.

Copyright © by **Shirley K. Higginbotham** 2024

Table of Contents

* **Chapter 1: From Zero to One: A Retrospective:** Review the key milestones and lessons learned during the initial startup phase. Analyze what worked, what didn't, and why.

* **Chapter 2: Defining Your "One":** Clearly articulate the core product, market, and competitive advantage that defines your current success.

* **Chapter 3: Financial Health Check:** Evaluate your current financial position, including revenue streams, profitability, and cash flow. Identify areas for improvement.

* **Chapter 4: Team Assessment:** Analyze your team's strengths and weaknesses. Identify skill gaps and potential leadership challenges as you scale.

* **Chapter 5: Market Analysis 2.0:** Re-evaluate your target market. Are there new segments to explore? How has the competitive landscape changed?

* **Chapter 6: Scaling Your Operations:** Discuss strategies for efficiently scaling operations, including manufacturing, logistics, customer service, and technology infrastructure.

* **Chapter 7: Strategic Partnerships:** Explore the benefits and challenges of forming strategic alliances to expand your reach and capabilities.

* **Chapter 8: Talent Acquisition and Retention:** Address the critical need for attracting and retaining top talent as your company grows. Discuss compensation, culture, and employee development.

* **Chapter 9: Funding and Capital:** Explore different funding options for scaling, including venture capital, private equity, and debt financing. Discuss the pros and cons of each.

* **Chapter 10: Marketing and Sales Strategies:** Develop strategies for scaling your marketing and sales efforts to reach a wider audience. Discuss different channels and approaches.

Chapter 11: Managing Growth Pains: Address common challenges associated with rapid growth, such as communication breakdowns, organizational inefficiencies, and cultural shifts.

* **Chapter 12: Innovation and Adaptation:** Discuss the importance of continuous innovation and adaptation to stay ahead of the competition.

* **Chapter 13: Leadership and Culture:** Explore the role of leadership in fostering a positive and productive company culture during periods of rapid growth.

* **Chapter 14: Measuring Success Beyond Revenue:** Define key performance indicators (KPIs) beyond revenue to track progress and ensure sustainable growth.

* **Chapter 15: The Future of Your Startup:** Conclude with a forward-looking perspective on the long-term vision and potential for your startup.

Conclusion: The Journey Continues

Chapter 1 From Zero to One: A Wild Ride (and What We Learned)

Okay, let's be honest, the first year of [Startup Name] was a rollercoaster. Think less "smooth ascent" and more "white-knuckle, stomach-churning freefall with occasional moments of pure exhilaration." We went from a couple of guys (and maybe a dog) huddled around a laptop to... well, something a little more organized (mostly). This chapter is all about looking back at that crazy first year, celebrating the wins, dissecting the epic fails, and figuring out what we can take with us as we try to actually *grow* this thing.

The Wild West: Those First Six Months

Picture this: ramen noodles for dinner, fueled by caffeine and sheer willpower. We launched our MVP – our Minimum Viable Product, for the uninitiated – with about as much fanfare as a whisper in a hurricane. But hey, we got feedback! And that feedback was... interesting. Turns out, our initial assumptions about who needed our product and *why* were, shall we say, a little off. We thought we were solving X problem, but it turned out people were actually struggling with Y. So, we pivoted. And pivoted again. And maybe pivoted one more time before we finally landed on something that kinda, sorta, maybe resonated.

Getting seed funding from [Angel Investor Name/VC Firm Name] was a huge win. Suddenly, we could afford more than ramen (hallelujah!). We hired some amazing people, and things started to feel... less chaotic. But then came the growing pains. More people meant more meetings, more emails, and more chances for things to fall through the cracks. We learned the hard way that clear communication isn't just a nice-to-have; it's a survival skill. We also discovered the power of project management tools – something we definitely should have implemented sooner.

The Valley of Despair (and a Few Pizza Parties): Months 6-12

Months six through twelve? Let's just call it "the valley of despair" with a few strategically placed pizza parties to keep morale up. We had some serious setbacks. Remember that time [mention a specific setback in a casual, relatable way, e.g., the server crashed during our biggest launch yet, a key feature was buggy as heck, a competitor stole our thunder]? Yeah, not our finest moments. But those setbacks forced us to get creative, to think outside the box, and to really question everything we thought we knew.

One of the biggest lessons we learned? Data is your friend. We started out relying on gut feelings and "vibes," which, let's be honest, isn't the most reliable strategy. We finally started tracking everything – user behavior, website traffic, conversion rates – and it was like flipping on a light switch. Suddenly, we could see what was working, what wasn't, and make informed decisions instead of just guessing.

The Light at the End of the Tunnel (and Maybe a Margarita): Months 12-18

By the end of the year, things started to look up. We hit some serious milestones: [mention specific achievements in a casual, relatable way, e.g., we finally cracked 10,000 users, landed a major partnership, became (slightly) profitable]. It felt amazing. Like, "we actually did it!" amazing. But with success came new challenges. We had to figure out how to scale without losing our sanity (or our company culture).

One thing that really helped us was focusing on our customers. We weren't just building a product; we were building relationships. We listened to their feedback, responded to their emails (even the grumpy ones), and tried our best to make them happy. It sounds cheesy, but it really made a difference. Loyal customers became our biggest advocates, and word-of-mouth marketing became our secret weapon.

The Big Takeaways (and Maybe a Nap):

So, what did we learn from this crazy first year? A few things:

* Gut feelings are great, but data is king:** Trust the numbers, not just your intuition.
* Flexibility is your superpower:** Be prepared to pivot, adapt, and change course when needed.
* Communication is everything:** Clear, consistent communication is crucial for a successful team.
* Customers are your best friends (and your best marketing team):** Treat them well, and they'll treat you well back.
* Celebrate the small wins:** Because those ramen noodle dinners were *rough*.

This first year was a wild ride, full of ups and downs, successes and failures. But it laid the foundation for everything that's to come. We're ready for the next chapter – scaling up and taking on new challenges. And hopefully, with a little less ramen and a lot more sleep.

Chapter 2 Defining Our "One": What We're REALLY Good At (and Why It Matters)

Okay, so we survived the first year. We're not exactly swimming in champagne yet, but we're definitely not eating ramen every night anymore. That's a win, right? But now it's time to get serious. We've got some traction, some happy customers, and maybe even a little bit of cash in the bank. But to truly *scale*, we need to be crystal clear on what we're actually doing, who we're doing it for, and why we're better than everyone else. In short, we need to define our "One."

Our Core Product: More Than Just a Widget

Let's talk about what we actually *make*. It's easy to get caught up in the technical details, the features, and the bells and whistles. But at its core, our product is [Clearly and concisely describe your core product, focusing on the value it provides to the customer. Avoid technical jargon. Example: "a simple, intuitive platform that helps small businesses manage their social media presence."].

It's not just about the features; it's about the *experience*. We've worked hard to create a product that is [Describe the user experience – easy to use, enjoyable, efficient, etc. Example: "easy to use, even for tech novices, and helps businesses save time and money."]. This focus on user experience is what sets us apart. It's not just about functionality; it's about making our users' lives easier and more productive.

Our Target Market: It's Not Everyone (and That's Okay)

We've learned the hard way that trying to be everything to everyone is a recipe for disaster. Our ideal customer is [Describe your ideal customer in detail. Include demographics, psychographics, needs, and pain points. Example: "a small business owner aged 30-50, who is tech-savvy but doesn't have a dedicated social media manager, and is struggling to manage their online presence effectively."].

This isn't just a demographic profile; it's a deep understanding of their needs, frustrations, and aspirations. We know their pain points, their challenges, and what keeps them up at night. This intimate understanding allows us to tailor our product and marketing messages to resonate deeply with our target audience. We're not trying to reach everyone; we're focusing on the people who will truly benefit from our product and become our most loyal advocates.

Our Competitive Advantage: Why Choose Us?

The market is crowded. There are plenty of other companies offering similar products or services. So, what makes us different? What's our secret sauce? Our competitive advantage is [Clearly articulate your competitive advantage. This could be based on price, features, technology, customer service, brand reputation, etc. Example: "our combination of ease of use, powerful features, and exceptional customer support."].

We're not just another widget in the marketplace. We offer [Explain what makes your product or service unique and superior to the competition. Example: "a personalized onboarding experience, proactive customer support, and a constantly evolving product roadmap based on user feedback."]. This commitment to excellence is what sets us apart and builds customer loyalty. It's not just about selling a product; it's about building a relationship.

Beyond the Features: The "Why" Behind Our "One"

Defining our "One" isn't just about listing features and target demographics. It's about understanding the deeper "why" behind our existence. Why did we start this company in the first place? What problem are we truly solving? What impact do we want to have on the world?

Our "why" is [Clearly articulate your company's mission and values. Example: "to empower small businesses to thrive in the digital age by providing them with the tools and support they need to succeed."]. This mission statement guides our decisions, shapes our culture, and inspires our team. It's the North Star that keeps us focused and motivated, even when things get tough.

Putting It All Together: Our "One" in Action

So, what does our "One" look like in practice? It's a combination of:

* A core product that solves a specific problem for our target market.
* A user experience that is intuitive, enjoyable, and efficient.
* A competitive advantage that sets us apart from the competition.
* A clear mission and values that guide our decisions and inspire our team.

Defining our "One" is not a one-time event; it's an ongoing process. As we grow and evolve, we'll need to revisit and refine our understanding of our core product, target market, and competitive advantage. But having a clear understanding of our "One" is essential for making informed decisions, allocating resources effectively, and building a sustainable and thriving business. It's the foundation upon which we'll build our future growth. And that's a pretty good place to be.

Chapter 3 Financial Health Check: Let's Talk Money (Because It Matters)

Okay, let's ditch the fluffy stuff for a minute and get down to brass tacks: money. We've built a great product, we've got some happy customers, but are we actually *making* money? And more importantly, are we *managing* our money effectively? This chapter is all about taking a hard look at our financial health, celebrating the wins, identifying the problem areas, and figuring out how to make our money work harder for us.

Revenue Streams: Where the Dough Comes From

First things first: where's the money coming from? We've got a few different revenue streams, and understanding each one is crucial.

*   **[Revenue Stream 1]:** [Describe your primary revenue stream. Example: "Our subscription model, where customers pay a monthly fee for access to our platform."]. This is our bread and butter, and it's been performing [Describe the performance of this revenue stream. Example: "relatively well, with steady growth over the past few months."]. However, we could improve [Identify areas for improvement. Example: "customer retention by implementing a more robust onboarding process and providing more personalized support."].

*   **[Revenue Stream 2]:** [Describe a secondary revenue stream, if applicable. Example: "Our premium features, which offer additional functionality for an extra fee."]. This revenue stream is [Describe the performance of this revenue stream. Example: "still relatively small, but showing promising growth potential."]. To boost this, we could [Identify areas for improvement. Example: "focus on marketing these features more effectively and highlighting their value proposition to our customers."].

*   **[Revenue Stream 3]:** [Describe any other revenue streams, if applicable. Example: "Partnerships with other businesses, where we receive a commission on sales."]. This is a [Describe the performance of this revenue stream. Example: "relatively new revenue stream, and we're still experimenting to find the most effective approach."]. We need to [Identify areas for improvement. Example: "focus on building stronger relationships with potential partners and developing more mutually beneficial agreements."].

Profitability: Are We Actually Making a Profit?

It's easy to get caught up in revenue numbers, but profitability is the real measure of success. Are we making more money than we're spending? Right now, our profit margin is [State your current profit margin]. This is [Describe whether this is good, bad, or needs improvement. Example: "not bad, but we could definitely do better."].

To improve our profitability, we need to focus on [Identify specific areas for improvement. Examples: "reducing our operating costs, increasing our revenue, or a combination of both."]. This might involve [Suggest specific actions. Examples: "negotiating better deals with our suppliers, streamlining our operations, or raising our prices strategically."].

Cash Flow: Keeping the Lights On

Cash flow is king, especially for startups. It's not enough to be profitable; we need to ensure we have enough cash on hand to cover our expenses. Our current cash flow is [Describe your current cash flow situation. Example: "relatively healthy, but we need to be mindful of our spending."].

To improve our cash flow, we need to [Identify specific areas for improvement. Examples: "improve our collection process, negotiate better payment terms with our suppliers, or secure additional funding."]. We also need to [Suggest specific actions. Examples: "create a more accurate cash flow forecast, monitor our expenses closely, and prioritize our spending."].

Areas for Improvement: Let's Get Real

Let's be honest, there's always room for improvement. Here are some key areas we need to focus on:

*   **Cost Optimization:** We need to find ways to reduce our operating costs without sacrificing quality. This might involve [Suggest specific actions. Examples: "negotiating better deals with our suppliers, streamlining our operations, or automating certain tasks."].

*   **Revenue Generation:** We need to explore new revenue streams and find ways to increase our sales. This might involve [Suggest specific actions. Examples: "expanding into new markets, developing new products, or improving our marketing efforts."].

*   **Pricing Strategy:** We need to ensure our pricing strategy is aligned with our target market and our cost structure. This might involve [Suggest specific actions. Examples: "raising our prices, offering different pricing tiers, or implementing a freemium model."].

*   **Financial Forecasting:** We need to develop more accurate financial forecasts to help us make better decisions about our spending and investment. This might involve [Suggest specific actions. Examples: "using more sophisticated financial modeling tools, consulting with a financial advisor, or improving our data collection and analysis."].

* **Financial Discipline:** We need to be more disciplined in our spending and ensure we're making smart investments. This might involve [Suggest specific actions. Examples: "creating a more detailed budget, tracking our expenses closely, and prioritizing our spending."].

This financial health check isn't about beating ourselves up; it's about being realistic, identifying areas for improvement, and developing a plan to achieve our financial goals. By focusing on these key areas, we can ensure that we're not just surviving, but thriving. And that, my friends, is what it's all about.

Chapter 4 Team Assessment: The Humans Behind the Hustle (and How to Make Them Awesome)

Okay, let's talk about the people – the amazing, sometimes frustrating, always essential humans who make this whole startup thing possible. We've come a long way from the initial "kitchen table" crew, and as we grow, it's crucial to take stock of our team's strengths, weaknesses, and potential challenges. This isn't about pointing fingers; it's about building a stronger, more effective team that can handle the challenges of scaling.

Strengths: What We're Already Rocking

Let's start with the good stuff. What are we already doing well? What are our team's superpowers?

*   **[Strength 1]: Innovation and Creativity:** We're a bunch of creative problem-solvers. We're not afraid to think outside the box, experiment with new ideas, and push the boundaries of what's possible. This has been crucial in developing our product and adapting to changing market conditions. We need to nurture this by [Suggest ways to nurture this strength. Example: "continuing to encourage brainstorming sessions, providing opportunities for professional development, and celebrating innovative solutions."].

*   **[Strength 2]: Collaboration and Teamwork:** We're a tight-knit team that works well together. We communicate openly, support each other, and are always willing to lend a hand. This collaborative spirit has been essential in overcoming challenges and achieving our goals. We can strengthen this by [Suggest ways to strengthen this strength. Example: "implementing team-building activities, fostering a culture of open communication, and recognizing and rewarding collaborative efforts."].

* **[Strength 3]: Adaptability and Resilience:** We've faced our share of setbacks, but we've always bounced back stronger. Our ability to adapt to changing circumstances and persevere through challenges has been crucial to our success. We can maintain this by [Suggest ways to maintain this strength. Example: "embracing a culture of learning from mistakes, providing support during challenging times, and celebrating successes, no matter how small."].

* **[Strength 4]: Customer Focus:** We're obsessed with our customers. We listen to their feedback, respond to their concerns, and strive to exceed their expectations. This customer-centric approach has been instrumental in building a loyal customer base. We can maintain this by [Suggest ways to maintain this strength. Example: "continuing to solicit customer feedback, providing exceptional customer service, and prioritizing customer needs in our product development process."].

Weaknesses: Areas for Improvement

Now for the less glamorous stuff: where do we need to improve? What are our blind spots? Honesty is key here.

* **[Weakness 1]: Communication Breakdown:** As we've grown, communication has become more challenging. Sometimes, information gets lost in translation, leading to misunderstandings and inefficiencies. We need to [Suggest solutions. Example: "implement better communication tools, establish clearer communication protocols, and schedule regular team meetings to ensure everyone is on the same page."].

* **[Weakness 2]: Lack of Specialization:** Some team members are wearing too many hats, leading to burnout and potential errors. We need to [Suggest solutions. Example: "hire additional staff to fill skill gaps, delegate tasks more effectively, and provide training to enhance individual skills."].

*   **[Weakness 3]: Process Inefficiencies:** Some of our internal processes are clunky and inefficient, leading to wasted time and resources. We need to [Suggest solutions. Example: "streamline our workflows, implement better project management tools, and automate repetitive tasks."].

*   **[Weakness 4]: Lack of Leadership Development:** As we scale, we'll need strong leaders at all levels. We need to [Suggest solutions. Example: "invest in leadership training programs, identify and develop potential leaders within the team, and create opportunities for leadership development."].

Skill Gaps: What We Need to Fill

What skills are missing from our team? What expertise do we need to acquire to support our growth?

*   **[Skill Gap 1]: Marketing Expertise:** We need someone with experience in [Specific marketing skill. Example: "digital marketing, social media marketing, or content marketing"]. This will help us [Explain the benefit of filling this skill gap. Example: "reach a wider audience, improve our brand awareness, and drive more sales."].

*   **[Skill Gap 2]: Technical Skills:** We need someone with expertise in [Specific technical skill. Example: "software development, data analysis, or cloud computing"]. This will help us [Explain the benefit of filling this skill gap. Example: "improve our product development process, enhance our data analysis capabilities, and improve the scalability of our infrastructure."].

* **[Skill Gap 3]: Financial Expertise:** We need someone with experience in [Specific financial skill. Example: "financial planning, budgeting, or financial analysis"]. This will help us [Explain the benefit of filling this skill gap. Example: "make better financial decisions, improve our cash flow management, and ensure the long-term financial health of the company."].

Leadership Challenges: Navigating the Growth Curve

Scaling brings leadership challenges. We need to [Suggest solutions to leadership challenges. Examples: "develop a clear leadership structure, establish clear roles and responsibilities, and provide leadership training to our team members."]. We also need to [Suggest solutions to leadership challenges. Examples: "foster a culture of open communication and collaboration, create opportunities for leadership development, and recognize and reward leadership contributions."].

This team assessment isn't about finding fault; it's about building a stronger, more effective team. By addressing our weaknesses, filling our skill gaps, and proactively addressing potential leadership challenges, we can ensure that our team is well-equipped to handle the challenges of scaling and achieve our ambitious goals. It's about empowering our team to be the best versions of themselves, and that's a win for everyone.

Chapter 5 Market Analysis 2.0: Checking the Rearview Mirror (and the Road Ahead)

Okay, we've survived the first year, celebrated some wins, and maybe even learned a thing or two. But the market? It's not standing still. Competitors are popping up like mushrooms after a rain shower, customer needs are evolving faster than we can keep up, and what worked yesterday might be completely irrelevant tomorrow. This chapter is all about taking a fresh look at our market – re-evaluating our target audience, exploring new opportunities, and understanding the ever-shifting competitive landscape.

Re-evaluating Our Target Market: Who Are We REALLY Serving?

Remember those initial assumptions we made about our target market? Yeah, let's revisit those. We thought we were serving [Describe your initial target market assumptions. Example: "small businesses with limited marketing budgets"]. And while that's still a part of our customer base, our experience over the past year has shown us that [Describe what you've learned about your target market. Example: "our product also resonates strongly with larger businesses that need a more efficient way to manage their social media presence."].

This means our target market is actually broader than we initially thought. We're not just serving [Describe your initial target market assumptions. Example: "small businesses with limited marketing budgets"]; we're also serving [Describe the expanded target market. Example: "larger businesses that need a more efficient way to manage their social media presence, as well as individuals who manage social media for multiple clients."]. This expanded market presents significant growth opportunities, but it also requires us to adapt our marketing and sales strategies to reach these new customer segments.

New Segments to Explore: Uncharted Territory

Now that we have a clearer understanding of our target market, let's explore some new segments. Are there any adjacent markets we could tap into? Are there any unmet needs we could address?

* **[New Segment 1]:** [Describe a potential new market segment. Example: "Non-profit organizations that need help managing their social media presence."]. This segment is attractive because [Explain why this segment is attractive. Example: "they have a strong need for our product, but they often have limited budgets, so we need to develop a pricing strategy that is both affordable and sustainable."].

* **[New Segment 2]:** [Describe another potential new market segment. Example: "Large corporations that need a more robust and scalable solution for managing their social media presence."]. This segment is attractive because [Explain why this segment is attractive. Example: "they have larger budgets and a greater need for our product, but they also have more complex requirements, so we need to develop a solution that is both scalable and customizable."].

* **[New Segment 3]:** [Describe another potential new market segment. Example: "International markets where there is a growing demand for our product."]. This segment is attractive because [Explain why this segment is attractive. Example: "it presents a significant opportunity for growth, but it also requires us to adapt our product and marketing messages to meet the specific needs and preferences of these markets."].

Exploring these new segments requires careful research and planning. We need to understand the specific needs and preferences of these customers, develop targeted marketing campaigns, and adapt our product to meet their requirements. But the potential rewards are significant.

The Competitive Landscape: Keeping an Eye on the Competition

The market isn't static. New competitors are constantly emerging, and existing competitors are constantly evolving. We need to keep a close eye on the competition to understand their strengths, weaknesses, and strategies.

*   **[Competitor 1]:** [Describe a key competitor. Example: "A large, established company with a wide range of social media management tools."]. Their strengths are [List their strengths. Example: "their brand recognition, their extensive feature set, and their large customer base."]. Their weaknesses are [List their weaknesses. Example: "their high price point, their complex user interface, and their lack of personalized customer support."]. We can compete by [Explain your competitive strategy. Example: "offering a more affordable and user-friendly product with exceptional customer support."].

*   **[Competitor 2]:** [Describe another key competitor. Example: "A smaller, more agile company with a focus on innovation."]. Their strengths are [List their strengths. Example: "their innovative features, their strong customer relationships, and their rapid product development cycle."]. Their weaknesses are [List their weaknesses. Example: "their limited resources, their lack of brand recognition, and their smaller customer base."]. We can compete by [Explain your competitive strategy. Example: "focusing on our core strengths, building strong customer relationships, and continuously innovating to stay ahead of the curve."].

*   **[Competitor 3]:** [Describe another key competitor. Example: "A new entrant with a disruptive technology."]. Their strengths are [List their strengths. Example: "their innovative technology, their low price point, and their aggressive marketing strategy."]. Their weaknesses are [List their weaknesses. Example: "their lack of brand recognition, their limited customer base, and their unproven track record."]. We can compete by [Explain your competitive strategy. Example: "highlighting our experience, our strong customer relationships, and our proven track record of success."].

Understanding the competitive landscape is crucial for making informed decisions about our product development, marketing, and sales strategies. By staying ahead of the curve and adapting to the changing market dynamics, we can maintain our competitive advantage and achieve our ambitious growth goals. It's a constant game of chess, but with a little foresight and a lot of hustle, we can stay ahead of the game.

Chapter 6 Scaling Our Operations: Growing Up Without Growing Old (or Breaking the Bank)

Okay, we've got a great product, happy customers, and a clearer picture of where we're headed. But now comes the real challenge: scaling. This isn't just about making more money; it's about building a sustainable, efficient operation that can handle significant growth without imploding under its own weight. This chapter is all about the nuts and bolts of scaling – from manufacturing and logistics to customer service and tech infrastructure – and how to do it smart, efficiently, and without breaking the bank.

Manufacturing (or Whatever We Actually *Make*): Keeping Up With Demand

Let's start with the basics: how do we actually produce our product (or service)? If we're a software company, this means scaling our development process. If we're a physical product company, this means scaling our manufacturing process. Either way, it's about finding ways to increase production without sacrificing quality or driving up costs.

*   **Streamlining Production:** We need to identify bottlenecks in our current production process and find ways to eliminate them. This might involve [Suggest specific actions. Examples: "automating repetitive tasks, improving our workflow, or investing in new equipment."]. The goal is to increase efficiency and reduce costs without compromising quality.

*   **Outsourcing:** For certain tasks, outsourcing might be a more cost-effective solution. This could involve [Suggest specific actions. Examples: "outsourcing manufacturing to a third-party supplier, outsourcing customer service to a call center, or outsourcing marketing to a marketing agency."]. However, it's crucial to choose reliable and reputable partners who share our values and commitment to quality.

*   **Strategic Partnerships:** Collaborating with other businesses can help us scale our operations more efficiently. This could involve [Suggest specific actions. Examples: "partnering with a distributor to expand our reach, partnering with a manufacturer to increase our production capacity, or partnering with a technology provider to improve our infrastructure."]. Strategic partnerships can provide access to resources, expertise, and markets that we might not have access to on our own.

Logistics: Getting Our Product to the Customer (Without Losing It)

Once we've produced our product, we need to get it to our customers. This is where logistics comes in. Efficient logistics are crucial for ensuring customer satisfaction and minimizing costs.

*   **Inventory Management:** We need to implement a robust inventory management system to ensure we have enough inventory on hand to meet demand without tying up too much capital. This might involve [Suggest specific actions. Examples: "using inventory management software, implementing a just-in-time inventory system, or forecasting demand more accurately."].

*   **Shipping and Delivery:** We need to choose reliable and cost-effective shipping and delivery partners. This might involve [Suggest specific actions. Examples: "negotiating better rates with our shipping carriers, optimizing our shipping routes, or using a third-party logistics provider."]. The goal is to get our product to our customers quickly, efficiently, and affordably.

*   **Supply Chain Management:** We need to manage our supply chain effectively to ensure we have access to the materials and resources we need to produce our product. This might involve [Suggest specific actions. Examples: "diversifying our suppliers, building strong relationships with our suppliers, or implementing a supply chain management system."]. A well-managed supply chain is crucial for ensuring the smooth flow of goods and minimizing disruptions.

Customer Service: Keeping Our Customers Happy (and Loyal)

Happy customers are loyal customers. As we scale, we need to ensure we can provide excellent customer service to all of our customers, regardless of their size or location.

*   **Scaling Our Support Team:** We need to expand our customer service team to handle the increased volume of inquiries. This might involve [Suggest specific actions. Examples: "hiring additional customer service representatives, implementing a knowledge base or FAQ section, or using a chatbot to handle common inquiries."]. The goal is to provide prompt, helpful, and personalized support to all of our customers.

*   **Improving Our Support Processes:** We need to streamline our customer service processes to ensure we can resolve issues quickly and efficiently. This might involve [Suggest specific actions. Examples: "implementing a ticketing system, using customer service software, or providing training to our customer service representatives."]. The goal is to provide a seamless and positive customer service experience.

*   **Proactive Customer Support:** We need to anticipate customer needs and proactively address potential issues. This might involve [Suggest specific actions. Examples: "monitoring customer feedback, proactively reaching out to customers who are having problems, or providing regular updates on our product development progress."]. Proactive customer support can help prevent problems before they arise and build stronger customer relationships.

Technology Infrastructure: The Backbone of Our Operation

Our technology infrastructure is the backbone of our operation. As we scale, we need to ensure our infrastructure can handle the increased load and provide a reliable and secure platform for our customers.

*   **Scalable Infrastructure:** We need to choose a technology infrastructure that can scale easily to meet our growing needs. This might involve [Suggest specific actions. Examples: "using cloud-based services, implementing a microservices architecture, or investing in high-capacity servers."]. A scalable infrastructure is crucial for ensuring the stability and performance of our platform.

*   **Security:** We need to implement robust security measures to protect our customers' data and our own intellectual property. This might involve [Suggest specific actions. Examples: "using encryption, implementing firewalls, or using intrusion detection systems."]. Security is paramount for maintaining customer trust and protecting our business.

* **Automation:** We need to automate as many tasks as possible to improve efficiency and reduce costs. This might involve [Suggest specific actions. Examples: "using automation tools, implementing robotic process automation, or using artificial intelligence."]. Automation can free up our team to focus on more strategic tasks.

Scaling our operations is a complex and ongoing process. By focusing on these key areas, we can build a sustainable, efficient, and profitable business that can handle significant growth. It's about building a strong foundation that can support our future success. And that's a pretty good feeling.

Chapter 7 Strategic Partnerships: Joining Forces to Conquer the World (or at Least a Bigger Slice of It)

Okay, we've got a solid foundation, we're growing steadily, but let's be honest: there's only so much we can do on our own. To truly scale and reach our full potential, we need to think bigger – and that means strategic partnerships. This chapter is all about exploring the exciting possibilities (and potential pitfalls) of joining forces with other companies to expand our reach, enhance our capabilities, and ultimately, conquer the market (or at least a much bigger slice of it).

Why Partner? The Benefits of Strategic Alliances

Let's start with the good stuff. Why bother with strategic partnerships in the first place? The benefits are numerous:

* **Expanded Reach:** Partnering with a company that has a larger customer base or a wider geographic reach can significantly expand our market penetration. Imagine suddenly having access to [Describe the potential benefits of expanded reach. Example: "thousands of new customers who are already familiar with our partner's brand and trust their recommendations."]. That's a game-changer.

* **Enhanced Capabilities:** Partnering with a company that has complementary skills or technologies can enhance our capabilities and allow us to offer a more comprehensive product or service. Think about [Describe the potential benefits of enhanced capabilities. Example: "integrating our platform with a popular CRM system, giving our customers a more seamless and integrated experience."]. This kind of synergy can be incredibly powerful.

*   **Reduced Costs:** Partnering can help us reduce costs by sharing resources, expertise, and infrastructure. Instead of building everything from scratch, we can leverage our partner's existing resources, saving us time and money. This means [Describe the potential benefits of reduced costs. Example: "we can focus our resources on product development and marketing, rather than building and maintaining our own infrastructure."]. That's a huge advantage.

*   **Increased Brand Awareness:** Partnering with a well-known brand can significantly increase our brand awareness and credibility. Suddenly, we're not just a small startup; we're associated with a respected and trusted brand. This means [Describe the potential benefits of increased brand awareness. Example: "we can reach a wider audience and build trust with potential customers who might not have otherwise considered our product."]. That's a powerful marketing boost.

*   **Access to New Markets:** Partnering with a company that operates in a different geographic region or market segment can help us expand into new territories and reach new customer groups. This opens up [Describe the potential benefits of access to new markets. Example: "a whole new world of opportunities, allowing us to diversify our revenue streams and reduce our reliance on a single market."]. That's a smart way to mitigate risk.

The Challenges: Navigating the Partnership Minefield

Of course, strategic partnerships aren't all sunshine and rainbows. There are potential challenges to consider:

* **Conflicting Goals:** Partners may have different goals and priorities, which can lead to conflicts and disagreements. It's crucial to establish clear goals and expectations from the outset and to ensure that both partners are aligned on the overall strategy. This requires [Describe the steps needed to avoid conflicting goals. Example: "open communication, clear agreements, and a shared vision for success."].

* **Cultural Differences:** Different companies have different cultures and ways of doing things. These cultural differences can lead to misunderstandings and communication breakdowns. To mitigate this, we need [Describe the steps needed to mitigate cultural differences. Example: "to foster a culture of mutual respect and understanding, to establish clear communication protocols, and to build strong personal relationships between team members."].

* **Loss of Control:** Partnering means sharing control and decision-making power. This can be challenging for companies that are used to operating independently. To address this, we need [Describe the steps needed to address loss of control. Example: "to clearly define roles and responsibilities, to establish a clear decision-making process, and to maintain open communication channels."].

* **Financial Risks:** Partnering involves financial risks, such as the potential for losses if the partnership fails. To mitigate these risks, we need [Describe the steps needed to mitigate financial risks. Example: "to conduct thorough due diligence on potential partners, to negotiate favorable terms, and to have a clear exit strategy in place."].

* **Legal and Contractual Issues:** Partnering involves legal and contractual issues, such as intellectual property rights, liability, and termination clauses. It's crucial to have a well-drafted contract that protects both partners' interests. This requires [Describe the steps needed to address legal and contractual issues. Example: "seeking legal counsel, negotiating favorable terms, and ensuring that the contract is clear, concise, and enforceable."].

Finding the Right Partner: A Match Made in Heaven (or at Least a Successful Business Venture)

Choosing the right partner is crucial for the success of any strategic alliance. We need to look for partners who:

* Share our values and vision.
* Have complementary skills and resources.
* Have a strong track record of success.
* Are financially stable and reliable.
* Are committed to a long-term partnership.

Finding the right partner takes time and effort, but it's an investment that can pay off handsomely. By carefully selecting our partners and managing the relationship effectively, we can leverage the power of strategic alliances to achieve our ambitious growth goals. It's about finding the right fit, building trust, and working together to achieve a common goal. And that, my friends, is a recipe for success.

Chapter 8 Talent Acquisition and Retention: Building a Dream Team (and Keeping Them Happy)

Okay, we've got a great product, a solid strategy, and some awesome partnerships. But none of that matters without the right people. As we scale, attracting and retaining top talent becomes absolutely critical. This isn't just about filling seats; it's about building a dream team – a group of passionate, skilled individuals who are not only incredibly talented but also genuinely excited to be part of our journey. This chapter is all about how to attract, retain, and develop that dream team.

Attracting Top Talent: Making Us the Employer of Choice

Let's be honest, the job market is competitive. Everyone wants the best people, so how do we make *us* the employer of choice?

* **Competitive Compensation:** Let's face it, money talks. We need to offer competitive salaries and benefits packages that attract top talent. This doesn't necessarily mean being the highest payer in the market, but it does mean being fair and competitive. We need to [Suggest specific actions. Examples: "research industry benchmarks, offer performance-based bonuses, and provide comprehensive health insurance."].

* **A Compelling Mission:** People want to work for companies that have a purpose. We need to articulate our mission clearly and passionately, showing potential employees how their work will make a difference. This means [Suggest specific actions. Examples: "highlighting our company values, showcasing our impact on the community, and emphasizing the positive impact of our work."].

* **A Positive Company Culture:** People want to work in a positive and supportive environment. We need to foster a culture of collaboration, respect, and open communication. This means [Suggest specific actions. Examples: "promoting teamwork, encouraging open feedback, and celebrating successes."].

* **Opportunities for Growth:** People want to feel like they're growing and learning. We need to provide opportunities for professional development, including training, mentorship, and advancement opportunities. This means [Suggest specific actions. Examples: "offering tuition reimbursement, providing mentorship programs, and creating clear career paths."].

* **Flexible Work Arrangements:** In today's world, flexibility is key. We need to offer flexible work arrangements, such as remote work options or flexible hours, to attract and retain top talent. This means [Suggest specific actions. Examples: "offering remote work options, allowing flexible work hours, and providing a supportive work-life balance."].

Retaining Top Talent: Keeping Our Dream Team Happy

Attracting top talent is only half the battle. We also need to keep them happy and engaged.

* **Regular Feedback and Recognition:** People want to know they're valued. We need to provide regular feedback, both positive and constructive, and recognize and reward employees for their contributions. This means [Suggest specific actions. Examples: "conducting regular performance reviews, providing opportunities for feedback, and celebrating successes."].

* **Opportunities for Advancement:** People want to feel like they're growing and progressing in their careers. We need to provide opportunities for advancement, including promotions, raises, and new challenges. This means [Suggest specific actions. Examples: "creating clear career paths, offering mentorship programs, and providing opportunities for professional development."].

* **Work-Life Balance:** People need time to recharge. We need to promote a healthy work-life balance, encouraging employees to take breaks, use their vacation time, and disconnect after work hours. This means [Suggest specific actions. Examples: "encouraging employees to take breaks, providing generous vacation time, and promoting a healthy work-life balance."].

* **Investment in Employee Well-being:** We need to invest in our employees' well-being, providing resources and support to help them manage stress, improve their mental health, and maintain a healthy lifestyle. This means [Suggest specific actions. Examples: "offering employee assistance programs, providing wellness initiatives, and promoting a healthy work environment."].

Employee Development: Investing in Our People

Investing in our employees' development is an investment in our future. We need to provide opportunities for our employees to learn and grow, both professionally and personally.

* **Training and Development Programs:** We need to offer training and development programs to help our employees enhance their skills and knowledge. This might involve [Suggest specific actions. Examples: "offering online courses, providing mentorship programs, or sending employees to conferences."].

*   **Mentorship Programs:** Mentorship programs can help employees develop their skills and advance their careers. This means [Suggest specific actions. Examples: "pairing experienced employees with newer employees, providing mentorship training, and creating a supportive mentorship culture."].

*   **Opportunities for Cross-Training:** Cross-training can help employees develop new skills and broaden their perspectives. This means [Suggest specific actions. Examples: "encouraging employees to take on new challenges, providing opportunities for cross-functional collaboration, and creating a culture of continuous learning."].

Building a dream team and keeping them happy is an ongoing process. It requires a commitment to providing competitive compensation, fostering a positive company culture, and investing in employee development. But the rewards are well worth the effort. A happy, engaged team is a productive team, and a productive team is the key to our long-term success. It's about building a team that's not just talented, but also passionate, engaged, and excited to be part of our journey. And that's a pretty amazing thing.

Chapter 9 Funding and Capital: Fueling the Rocket (Without Blowing Up the Engine)

Okay, we've got a great team, a solid strategy, and a growing customer base. But to truly scale, we need fuel – and that fuel comes in the form of capital. This chapter is all about exploring different funding options for scaling our business, weighing the pros and cons of each, and ultimately, choosing the right fuel for our rocket. The goal? To reach escape velocity without blowing up the engine.

Venture Capital (VC): The High-Stakes Gamble

Venture capital is often seen as the holy grail of startup funding. VC firms invest in high-growth companies in exchange for equity, typically a significant stake in the company. This can provide a huge injection of capital, allowing us to rapidly scale our operations.

Pros:

* **Significant Capital:** VC firms can provide substantial funding, allowing us to pursue ambitious growth plans.
* **Expertise and Mentorship:** VC firms often provide more than just money; they also offer valuable expertise and mentorship, helping us navigate the challenges of scaling.
* **Network and Connections:** VC firms have extensive networks and connections, which can help us access new markets, partners, and talent.
* **Validation:** Securing VC funding is a significant validation of our business model and potential.

Cons:

* **Loss of Control:** VC firms typically require a significant equity stake in exchange for their investment, which can dilute our ownership and reduce our control over the company.

*   **High Expectations:** VC firms have high expectations for growth and returns, which can put pressure on the management team.
*   **Potential for Conflicts:** Disagreements can arise between the management team and the VC firm regarding strategy and decision-making.
*   **Dilution:** Each round of funding dilutes the ownership of existing shareholders.

Private Equity (PE): The More Mature Option

Private equity is similar to venture capital, but it typically focuses on more mature companies with a proven track record. PE firms invest in companies in exchange for equity, often with the goal of improving the company's operations and eventually selling it for a profit.

Pros:

*   **Significant Capital:** PE firms can provide substantial funding, allowing us to pursue ambitious growth plans.
*   **Operational Expertise:** PE firms often have extensive operational expertise, which can help us improve our efficiency and profitability.
*   **Strategic Guidance:** PE firms can provide strategic guidance, helping us make informed decisions about our future direction.
*   **Exit Strategy:** PE firms often have a clear exit strategy, which can provide a path for us to eventually sell the company.

Cons:

*   **Loss of Control:** PE firms typically require a significant equity stake in exchange for their investment, which can dilute our ownership and reduce our control over the company.

*   **High Expectations:** PE firms have high expectations for growth and returns, which can put pressure on the management team.
*   **Potential for Conflicts:** Disagreements can arise between the management team and the PE firm regarding strategy and decision-making.
*   **Debt Burden:** PE firms may leverage debt to finance their acquisitions, which can increase the company's financial risk.

Debt Financing: Borrowing to Grow

Debt financing involves borrowing money from a lender, such as a bank or other financial institution. This can be a less dilutive way to raise capital, but it comes with the responsibility of repaying the loan with interest.

Pros:

*   **Less Dilutive:** Debt financing does not dilute our ownership, allowing us to retain more control over the company.
*   **Tax Deductible:** Interest payments on debt are typically tax deductible, which can reduce our tax burden.
*   **Flexibility:** Debt financing can offer more flexibility than equity financing, allowing us to tailor the terms of the loan to our specific needs.

Cons:

*   **Repayment Obligations:** We are obligated to repay the loan with interest, which can put a strain on our cash flow.
*   **Interest Costs:** Interest payments can significantly increase our overall costs.
*   **Collateral:** Lenders may require collateral, such as assets or personal guarantees, to secure the loan.
*   **Limited Funding:** Debt financing may not provide as much capital as equity financing.

Choosing the Right Fuel: A Personalized Approach

The best funding option for us will depend on our specific circumstances, including our stage of growth, our risk tolerance, and our long-term goals. There's no one-size-fits-all answer. We need to carefully consider the pros and cons of each option and choose the one that best aligns with our needs. This requires [Suggest specific actions. Examples: "conducting thorough due diligence, negotiating favorable terms, and seeking advice from experienced advisors."].

Ultimately, securing the right funding is crucial for scaling our business. It's about finding the right fuel to power our rocket, allowing us to reach escape velocity and achieve our ambitious goals. It's a strategic decision that requires careful planning, thorough research, and a clear understanding of our own needs and risk tolerance. And that's a journey worth taking.

Chapter 10 Marketing and Sales Strategies: Getting the Word Out (and Making the Sales)

Okay, we've got a great product, a solid team, and the funding to fuel our growth. But none of that matters if nobody knows about us. This chapter is all about scaling our marketing and sales efforts – reaching a wider audience, generating leads, and ultimately, making the sales that will drive our growth. It's about getting the word out in a smart, efficient, and effective way.

Scaling Our Marketing Efforts: Reaching a Wider Audience

Our initial marketing efforts might have been focused on a small, niche audience. But as we scale, we need to reach a much wider audience. This requires a multi-channel approach, leveraging a variety of marketing channels to reach our target customers where they are.

*   **Digital Marketing:** Digital marketing is essential for reaching a wide audience online. This includes:

    *   **Search Engine Optimization (SEO):** Optimizing our website and content for search engines to improve our organic search rankings. This means [Suggest specific actions. Examples: "conducting keyword research, creating high-quality content, and building backlinks."].

    *   **Pay-Per-Click (PPC) Advertising:** Running targeted advertising campaigns on search engines and social media platforms. This means [Suggest specific actions. Examples: "defining our target audience, setting a budget, and tracking our results."].

* **Social Media Marketing:** Building a strong presence on social media platforms to engage with our target audience and build brand awareness. This means [Suggest specific actions. Examples: "creating engaging content, running contests and giveaways, and interacting with our followers."].

* **Email Marketing:** Building an email list and sending targeted email campaigns to nurture leads and drive sales. This means [Suggest specific actions. Examples: "creating compelling email content, segmenting our email list, and tracking our results."].

* **Content Marketing:** Creating high-quality content, such as blog posts, articles, videos, and infographics, to attract and engage our target audience. This means [Suggest specific actions. Examples: "conducting keyword research, creating compelling content, and promoting our content on social media."].

* **Public Relations (PR):** Building relationships with journalists and bloggers to secure media coverage and build brand awareness. This means [Suggest specific actions. Examples: "developing a media kit, pitching stories to journalists, and building relationships with bloggers."].

* **Partnerships:** Collaborating with other businesses to reach a wider audience and build brand awareness. This means [Suggest specific actions. Examples: "identifying potential partners, negotiating partnerships, and promoting our partnerships on social media."].

Scaling Our Sales Efforts: Generating Leads and Closing Deals

Generating leads and closing deals is crucial for driving revenue growth. As we scale, we need to implement efficient sales processes and leverage different sales channels to reach our target customers.

* **Inbound Sales:** Attracting customers through our marketing efforts, such as content marketing, SEO, and social media marketing. This means [Suggest specific actions. Examples: "creating high-quality content, optimizing our website for search engines, and building a strong social media presence."].

* **Outbound Sales:** Proactively reaching out to potential customers through cold calling, email marketing, and social media outreach. This means [Suggest specific actions. Examples: "developing a sales script, identifying potential customers, and tracking our results."].

* **Sales Automation:** Using sales automation tools to streamline our sales processes and improve efficiency. This means [Suggest specific actions. Examples: "using CRM software, implementing email marketing automation, and using sales analytics dashboards."].

* **Sales Training:** Providing sales training to our sales team to enhance their skills and knowledge. This means [Suggest specific actions. Examples: "offering sales training courses, providing mentorship programs, and creating a supportive sales culture."].

* **Sales Enablement:** Providing our sales team with the tools and resources they need to be successful. This means [Suggest specific actions. Examples: "providing sales collateral, creating sales presentations, and providing access to sales training materials."].

Choosing the Right Channels and Approaches:

The best marketing and sales channels and approaches will depend on our target audience, our budget, and our overall marketing and sales strategy. We need to carefully analyze our target audience, understand their needs and preferences, and choose the channels and approaches that are most likely to reach them effectively. This requires [Suggest specific actions. Examples: "conducting market research, analyzing our target audience, and testing different channels and approaches."].

Scaling our marketing and sales efforts is an ongoing process. It requires a commitment to continuous improvement, experimentation, and adaptation. By constantly monitoring our results, analyzing our data, and making adjustments as needed, we can ensure that our marketing and sales strategies are effective and efficient. It's about finding the right mix of channels and approaches, optimizing our campaigns, and constantly striving to improve our results. And that's a recipe for sustainable growth.

Chapter 11 Managing Growth Pains: Navigating the Rapids Without Capsizing

Okay, we're scaling! Things are moving fast, and that's awesome. But rapid growth also brings its own set of challenges – what we affectionately call "growth pains." These aren't necessarily bad; they're just a natural part of the process. But if we don't address them proactively, they can quickly derail our progress. This chapter is all about identifying and managing those common growth pains – from communication breakdowns to cultural shifts – so we can navigate the rapids without capsizing.

Communication Breakdowns: The Tower of Babel Syndrome

As we grow, communication becomes increasingly complex. What worked when we were a small team might not work anymore. We might experience:

* **Information Silos:** Different departments or teams might not be sharing information effectively, leading to misunderstandings and inefficiencies. To combat this, we need [Suggest specific actions. Examples: "implement better communication tools, establish cross-functional communication channels, and encourage open communication across departments."].

* **Lack of Transparency:** Employees might not be kept informed about important company decisions or changes, leading to anxiety and uncertainty. To address this, we need [Suggest specific actions. Examples: "increase transparency by regularly communicating company updates, holding town hall meetings, and providing regular feedback to employees."].

* **Miscommunication:** Misunderstandings can arise due to poor communication, leading to errors and delays. To prevent this, we need [Suggest specific actions. Examples: "establish clear communication protocols, provide training on effective communication, and encourage open and honest communication."].

* **Overwhelmed Communication Channels:** Too many communication channels can lead to information overload and confusion. To streamline communication, we need [Suggest specific actions. Examples: "consolidate communication channels, establish clear guidelines for using different channels, and encourage employees to use the most appropriate channel for each communication."].

Organizational Inefficiencies: The Bottleneck Blues

Rapid growth can expose inefficiencies in our organizational structure and processes. We might experience:

* **Lack of Clear Roles and Responsibilities:** As we add new roles and responsibilities, it's crucial to ensure that everyone understands their role and how it contributes to the overall goals. To address this, we need [Suggest specific actions. Examples: "create clear job descriptions, establish clear reporting structures, and provide regular training on roles and responsibilities."].

* **Slow Decision-Making:** As the organization grows, decision-making can become slower and more cumbersome. To improve decision-making, we need [Suggest specific actions. Examples: "delegate decision-making authority, establish clear decision-making processes, and empower employees to make decisions."].

*   **Lack of Process Standardization:** Inconsistent processes can lead to errors, delays, and inefficiencies. To standardize processes, we need [Suggest specific actions. Examples: "document our processes, implement process improvement methodologies, and provide training on standardized processes."].

*   **Lack of Scalable Systems:** Our existing systems and infrastructure might not be able to handle the increased workload. To address this, we need [Suggest specific actions. Examples: "invest in new systems and infrastructure, upgrade our existing systems, and implement cloud-based solutions."].

Cultural Shifts: Maintaining Our Identity in the Face of Growth

Rapid growth can lead to significant cultural shifts, potentially impacting employee morale and productivity. We might experience:

*   **Loss of Company Culture:** As we grow, it's important to maintain our company culture and values. To preserve our culture, we need [Suggest specific actions. Examples: "reinforce our company values, celebrate successes, and create opportunities for employees to connect with each other."].

*   **Increased Competition:** As the company grows, competition for resources and opportunities can increase, potentially leading to conflict and resentment. To address this, we need [Suggest specific actions. Examples: "promote collaboration, establish clear guidelines for resource allocation, and create a culture of fairness and equity."].

*   **Decreased Employee Engagement:** Rapid growth can lead to decreased employee engagement if employees feel overwhelmed, undervalued, or disconnected from the company's mission. To improve employee engagement, we need [Suggest specific actions. Examples: "provide regular feedback, recognize and reward employees, and create opportunities for professional development."].

*   **Onboarding Challenges:** Onboarding new employees effectively becomes more challenging as the company grows. To improve onboarding, we need [Suggest specific actions. Examples: "develop a comprehensive onboarding program, provide regular training, and assign mentors to new employees."].

Proactive Management: Staying Ahead of the Curve

Managing growth pains requires a proactive approach. We need to anticipate potential challenges, develop strategies to address them, and continuously monitor our progress. This means:

*   **Regular Check-ins:** Regularly assess our progress, identify potential problems, and develop strategies to address them.
*   **Open Communication:** Maintain open communication channels to keep employees informed and engaged.
*   **Employee Feedback:** Solicit regular feedback from employees to identify areas for improvement.
*   **Continuous Improvement:** Continuously strive to improve our processes and systems to enhance efficiency and productivity.

Managing growth pains is an ongoing process. It requires a commitment to continuous improvement, open communication, and a willingness to adapt and change. But by proactively addressing these challenges, we can ensure that our growth is sustainable and that we can continue to thrive. It's about navigating the rapids without capsizing, and that's a journey worth taking.

Chapter 12 Innovation and Adaptation: The Only Constant is Change (and We Need to Embrace It)

Okay, we've made it! We've scaled, we're growing, and things are looking good. But the business world is a dynamic place, and what worked yesterday might not work tomorrow. To stay ahead of the competition and maintain our edge, we need to embrace continuous innovation and adaptation. This chapter is all about staying agile, embracing change, and constantly evolving to meet the ever-changing demands of the market.

The Importance of Continuous Innovation:

In today's fast-paced business environment, standing still is the same as falling behind. Continuous innovation is no longer a luxury; it's a necessity for survival. It's about:

* **Staying Ahead of the Curve:** By constantly innovating, we can stay ahead of the competition and maintain our competitive advantage. This means [Suggest specific actions. Examples: "investing in research and development, exploring new technologies, and developing new products and services."].

* **Meeting Evolving Customer Needs:** Customer needs are constantly evolving, and we need to adapt our products and services to meet those changing needs. This means [Suggest specific actions. Examples: "conducting market research, soliciting customer feedback, and iterating on our products and services based on that feedback."].

* **Creating New Opportunities:** Innovation can create new opportunities for growth and expansion. This means [Suggest specific actions. Examples: "exploring new markets, developing new business models, and creating new revenue streams."].

*   **Maintaining Relevance:** In a rapidly changing market, it's crucial to stay relevant and maintain our position as a leader in our industry. This means [Suggest specific actions. Examples: "staying informed about industry trends, adapting to changing market conditions, and continuously improving our products and services."].

Strategies for Continuous Innovation:

Continuous innovation doesn't just happen; it requires a deliberate and strategic approach. We need to:

*   **Foster a Culture of Innovation:** Create a company culture that encourages creativity, experimentation, and risk-taking. This means [Suggest specific actions. Examples: "encouraging employees to share ideas, providing resources for innovation, and celebrating successes."].

*   **Invest in Research and Development (R&D):** Allocate resources to research and development to explore new technologies and develop new products and services. This means [Suggest specific actions. Examples: "setting a budget for R&D, hiring skilled researchers and developers, and establishing clear goals for R&D."].

*   **Embrace Agile Methodologies:** Adopt agile methodologies to improve our ability to adapt to changing market conditions and customer needs. This means [Suggest specific actions. Examples: "using agile project management tools, implementing iterative development processes, and embracing a culture of continuous improvement."].

*   **Solicit Customer Feedback:** Regularly solicit customer feedback to understand their needs and preferences and to identify areas for improvement. This means [Suggest specific actions. Examples: "conducting surveys, conducting focus groups, and monitoring social media for customer feedback."].

*   **Monitor Industry Trends:** Stay informed about industry trends and emerging technologies to identify potential opportunities and threats. This means [Suggest specific actions. Examples: "reading industry publications, attending industry events, and networking with industry experts."].

The Importance of Adaptation:

Adaptation is just as crucial as innovation. It's about being flexible, responsive, and willing to change course when necessary. This means:

*   **Responding to Market Changes:** Quickly adapt to changes in the market, such as shifts in customer demand or the emergence of new competitors. This means [Suggest specific actions. Examples: "monitoring market trends, analyzing competitor activity, and adjusting our strategies accordingly."].

*   **Embracing New Technologies:** Be willing to embrace new technologies to improve our efficiency and effectiveness. This means [Suggest specific actions. Examples: "investing in new technologies, providing training to employees on new technologies, and integrating new technologies into our workflows."].

*   **Learning from Mistakes:** View mistakes as learning opportunities and use them to improve our processes and strategies. This means [Suggest specific actions. Examples: "conducting post-mortems, analyzing failures, and implementing corrective actions."].

*   **Being Flexible and Agile:** Maintain a flexible and agile organizational structure to adapt quickly to changing circumstances. This means [Suggest specific actions. Examples: "empowering employees to make decisions, establishing clear communication channels, and fostering a culture of collaboration."].

Building a Culture of Continuous Improvement:

Continuous innovation and adaptation require a culture of continuous improvement. This means:

*   **Setting Clear Goals:** Establish clear goals for innovation and adaptation, and track our progress regularly.
*   **Measuring Results:** Measure the results of our innovation and adaptation efforts to identify what's working and what's not.
*   **Iterating and Improving:** Continuously iterate on our products, services, and processes based on our results.
*   **Celebrating Successes:** Celebrate successes, both big and small, to encourage continuous improvement.

Continuous innovation and adaptation are not just about staying ahead of the competition; they're about creating a sustainable and thriving business. It's about embracing change, learning from our mistakes, and constantly striving to improve. And that's a journey worth taking. It's about building a culture of continuous improvement, where innovation and adaptation are not just buzzwords, but integral parts of our DNA. And that's what will keep us ahead of the game.

Chapter 13 Leadership and Culture: Steering the Ship Through Stormy Seas (and Keeping the Crew Happy)

Okay, we've conquered scaling, navigated the growth pains, and embraced innovation. But even with all that, success hinges on one crucial element: leadership. And not just any leadership; leadership that fosters a positive and productive company culture, especially during those intense periods of rapid growth. This chapter is all about the crucial role of leadership in steering the ship through stormy seas and keeping the crew happy, engaged, and rowing in the same direction.

The Importance of Strong Leadership During Growth:

Rapid growth brings unique challenges. The familiar comfort of a small, close-knit team is replaced by a larger, more complex organization. This is where strong leadership becomes absolutely critical. Effective leaders during this phase:

*   **Set a Clear Vision:** They articulate a clear and compelling vision for the future, providing direction and purpose for the entire organization. This means [Suggest specific actions. Examples: "clearly defining the company's mission, vision, and values, communicating this vision effectively to all employees, and ensuring that all decisions align with the overall vision."].

*   **Build a Strong Team:** They build a strong and cohesive team by attracting, retaining, and developing top talent. This means [Suggest specific actions. Examples: "creating a positive and supportive work environment, providing opportunities for professional development, and recognizing and rewarding employee contributions."].

*   **Foster Open Communication:** They create a culture of open communication, ensuring that information flows freely throughout the organization. This means [Suggest specific actions. Examples: "establishing clear communication channels, encouraging open feedback, and actively listening to employee concerns."].

*   **Empower Employees:** They empower employees to take ownership of their work and make decisions, fostering a sense of responsibility and accountability. This means [Suggest specific actions. Examples: "delegating authority, providing employees with the resources they need to succeed, and trusting them to make decisions."].

*   **Manage Change Effectively:** They manage change effectively, guiding the organization through periods of transition and uncertainty. This means [Suggest specific actions. Examples: "communicating changes clearly and transparently, providing support to employees during periods of change, and celebrating successes."].

*   **Promote Collaboration:** They promote collaboration and teamwork, breaking down silos and fostering a sense of unity and purpose. This means [Suggest specific actions. Examples: "creating opportunities for cross-functional collaboration, encouraging teamwork, and celebrating successes."].

Fostering a Positive and Productive Company Culture:

A positive and productive company culture is essential for attracting and retaining top talent, driving innovation, and achieving sustainable growth. Leaders play a crucial role in shaping this culture by:

*   **Defining Core Values:** Clearly defining and communicating the company's core values, ensuring that all employees understand and embrace them. This means [Suggest specific actions. Examples: "developing a clear statement of values, incorporating values into all aspects of the business, and recognizing and rewarding employees who embody those values."].

*   **Promoting Inclusivity:** Creating a diverse and inclusive workplace where all employees feel valued, respected, and empowered. This means [Suggest specific actions. Examples: "implementing diversity and inclusion initiatives, providing training on diversity and inclusion, and creating a culture of respect and understanding."].

*   **Encouraging Work-Life Balance:** Promoting a healthy work-life balance, ensuring that employees have time to recharge and avoid burnout. This means [Suggest specific actions. Examples: "offering flexible work arrangements, providing generous vacation time, and promoting a healthy work environment."].

*   **Recognizing and Rewarding Employees:** Regularly recognizing and rewarding employees for their contributions, fostering a sense of appreciation and motivation. This means [Suggest specific actions. Examples: "implementing a performance recognition program, providing opportunities for advancement, and celebrating successes."].

*   **Investing in Employee Development:** Investing in employee development, providing opportunities for training, mentorship, and career advancement. This means [Suggest specific actions. Examples: "offering tuition reimbursement, providing mentorship programs, and creating clear career paths."].

Leadership Styles and Growth:

Different leadership styles can be more or less effective during periods of rapid growth. While a highly directive style might be necessary in the early stages, a more collaborative and empowering style often becomes more effective as the company scales. Leaders need to be adaptable and adjust their style as needed. This means:

* **Adaptability:** Leaders need to be adaptable and adjust their leadership style as the company grows and changes.
* **Delegation:** Leaders need to effectively delegate tasks and responsibilities to empower employees.
* **Trust:** Leaders need to trust their employees to make decisions and take ownership of their work.
* **Communication:** Leaders need to maintain open and transparent communication with their employees.
* **Mentorship:** Leaders need to provide mentorship and guidance to their employees.

Building a Strong Leadership Team:

As the company grows, it's crucial to build a strong leadership team that can effectively manage the organization and guide it through periods of rapid growth. This means:

* **Identifying and Developing Leaders:** Identify and develop potential leaders within the organization, providing them with opportunities for training and development.
* **Creating a Leadership Pipeline:** Create a leadership pipeline to ensure that there is a succession plan in place.
* **Promoting Collaboration:** Encourage collaboration and teamwork among leaders.
* **Accountability:** Hold leaders accountable for their performance and results.

Leadership is the cornerstone of a thriving company culture, especially during periods of rapid growth. It's about setting a clear vision, building a strong team, fostering open communication, and empowering employees. It's about creating a positive and productive work environment where everyone feels valued, respected, and motivated. And that's the key to navigating the stormy seas of rapid growth and emerging stronger on the other side. It's about building a leadership team that's not just capable, but also collaborative, adaptable, and committed to fostering a culture of success. And that's a recipe for long-term growth and prosperity.

Chapter 14 Measuring Success Beyond Revenue: It's Not Just About the Benjamins

Okay, we all know revenue is important. It's the lifeblood of any business. But focusing *only* on revenue can be short-sighted. True, sustainable growth requires a broader perspective, measuring success beyond just the Benjamins. This chapter is all about defining key performance indicators (KPIs) that go beyond revenue, providing a more holistic view of our progress and ensuring we're building a truly successful and sustainable business.

Why Revenue Alone Isn't Enough:

While revenue is a crucial metric, relying solely on it can be misleading. A spike in revenue might mask underlying problems, such as:

*   **Unsustainable Growth:** Rapid revenue growth might be fueled by unsustainable practices, such as aggressive discounting or unsustainable marketing spend. This can lead to long-term problems.

*   **Poor Customer Retention:** High revenue might be masking poor customer retention. Acquiring new customers is expensive; retaining existing ones is far more efficient and profitable.

*   **Ignoring Other Key Areas:** Focusing solely on revenue can lead us to neglect other crucial areas of the business, such as employee satisfaction, product development, and brand building. These are all vital for long-term success.

*   **Short-Term Gains, Long-Term Pains:** Chasing short-term revenue gains can lead to long-term problems, such as damaging our brand reputation or alienating our customers.

KPIs Beyond Revenue: A More Holistic View

To get a more complete picture of our success, we need to track a range of KPIs that reflect different aspects of our business. These can be broadly categorized into:

1. Customer-centric KPIs: These metrics focus on customer satisfaction, loyalty, and lifetime value.

* **Customer Acquisition Cost (CAC):** How much does it cost to acquire a new customer? Lower CAC indicates efficient marketing and sales efforts.

* **Customer Lifetime Value (CLTV):** How much revenue will a customer generate over their relationship with us? Higher CLTV indicates strong customer loyalty and retention.

* **Customer Churn Rate:** What percentage of our customers cancel their subscriptions or stop doing business with us? Lower churn indicates strong customer satisfaction and retention.

* **Net Promoter Score (NPS):** How likely are our customers to recommend us to others? Higher NPS indicates strong brand loyalty and advocacy.

* **Customer Satisfaction (CSAT):** How satisfied are our customers with our products and services? Higher CSAT indicates strong customer satisfaction and loyalty.

2. Operational Efficiency KPIs: These metrics focus on the efficiency and effectiveness of our operations.

* **Average Order Value (AOV):** How much do customers spend on average per order? Higher AOV indicates effective upselling and cross-selling strategies.

* **Conversion Rate:** What percentage of website visitors or leads convert into paying customers? Higher conversion rates indicate effective marketing and sales funnels.

* **Website Traffic:** How many people are visiting our website? Higher website traffic indicates strong brand awareness and online visibility.

* **Marketing ROI:** What is the return on investment for our marketing efforts? Higher ROI indicates effective marketing spend.

* **Employee Turnover Rate:** What percentage of our employees leave the company each year? Lower turnover indicates strong employee satisfaction and retention.

3. Product Development KPIs: These metrics focus on the success of our product development efforts.

* **Time to Market:** How long does it take to develop and launch a new product or feature? Shorter time to market indicates efficient product development processes.

* **Product Adoption Rate:** What percentage of our customers are using a new product or feature? Higher adoption rates indicate successful product launches.

* **Bug Fix Rate:** How many bugs are being reported and fixed? Lower bug fix rates indicate high-quality product development.

* **Customer Feedback on New Features:** What is the customer feedback on new features? Positive feedback indicates successful product development.

4. Financial Health KPIs (Beyond Revenue):

*   **Profit Margin:** What percentage of our revenue is profit? Higher profit margins indicate efficient cost management.

*   **Burn Rate:** How much cash are we spending each month? Lower burn rate indicates efficient cash management.

*   **Debt-to-Equity Ratio:** What is the ratio of our debt to our equity? Lower debt-to-equity ratio indicates lower financial risk.

Building a Balanced Scorecard:

Instead of focusing solely on revenue, we should build a balanced scorecard that tracks a range of KPIs across different areas of the business. This provides a more holistic view of our progress and helps us identify areas for improvement. This means:

*   **Defining Key Metrics:** Clearly define the KPIs that are most relevant to our business goals.

*   **Setting Targets:** Set realistic and achievable targets for each KPI.

*   **Tracking Progress:** Regularly track our progress against our targets and make adjustments as needed.

*   **Analyzing Results:** Analyze our results to identify areas for improvement and to inform our future strategies.

Measuring success beyond revenue is crucial for building a sustainable and thriving business. It's about taking a holistic view of our progress, identifying areas for improvement, and making data-driven decisions. By tracking a range of KPIs, we can gain a more complete understanding of our performance and ensure that we're building a truly successful and sustainable business. It's about looking beyond the immediate numbers and focusing on the long-term health and sustainability of our business. And that's a strategy that will pay off in the long run.

Chapter 15 The Future of Your Startup: Reaching for the Stars (and Actually Getting There)

We've come a long way. From a humble beginning, we've built a thriving business, navigated the challenges of scaling, and established a strong foundation for future growth. But the journey doesn't end here. This final chapter is about looking ahead – envisioning the future of our startup, outlining our long-term vision, and exploring the incredible potential that lies ahead. It's about reaching for the stars and, this time, actually getting there.

Our Long-Term Vision: More Than Just a Business

Our long-term vision goes beyond simply making money. It's about building something meaningful, something that makes a real difference in the world. This means:

* **Defining Our Legacy:** What kind of impact do we want to have on the world? What do we want to be remembered for? This requires [Suggest specific actions. Examples: "clearly articulating our mission and values, defining our long-term goals, and ensuring that all our actions align with our vision."].

* **Setting Ambitious Goals:** Setting ambitious but achievable goals that will challenge us and push us to reach our full potential. This means [Suggest specific actions. Examples: "defining specific, measurable, achievable, relevant, and time-bound (SMART) goals, regularly reviewing our progress, and adjusting our goals as needed."].

* **Building a Sustainable Business:** Building a sustainable business that can withstand economic downturns and continue to thrive for years to come. This means [Suggest specific actions. Examples: "diversifying our revenue streams, managing our finances responsibly, and building strong relationships with our customers and partners."].

*   **Creating a Positive Impact:** Creating a positive impact on the world, whether through our products, services, or our company culture. This means [Suggest specific actions. Examples: "supporting charitable causes, promoting sustainability, and creating a positive work environment."].

Potential for Growth and Expansion:

The potential for growth and expansion is immense. We can:

*   **Expand into New Markets:** Expand into new geographic markets or target new customer segments. This requires [Suggest specific actions. Examples: "conducting market research, developing targeted marketing campaigns, and adapting our products and services to meet the needs of new markets."].

*   **Develop New Products and Services:** Develop new products and services to expand our offerings and meet evolving customer needs. This requires [Suggest specific actions. Examples: "investing in research and development, soliciting customer feedback, and iterating on our products and services based on that feedback."].

*   **Strategic Acquisitions:** Acquire complementary businesses to expand our capabilities and market share. This requires [Suggest specific actions. Examples: "conducting due diligence, negotiating favorable terms, and integrating acquired businesses effectively."].

*   **Strategic Partnerships:** Form strategic partnerships to expand our reach and capabilities. This requires [Suggest specific actions. Examples: "identifying potential partners, negotiating partnerships, and promoting our partnerships effectively."].

Challenges and Opportunities:

While the potential for growth is significant, we also need to be aware of the challenges that lie ahead. These include:

* **Competition:** The competitive landscape is constantly evolving, and we need to stay ahead of the curve. This requires [Suggest specific actions. Examples: "monitoring competitor activity, innovating continuously, and adapting to changing market conditions."].

* **Economic Uncertainty:** Economic downturns can impact our business, and we need to be prepared for these challenges. This requires [Suggest specific actions. Examples: "managing our finances responsibly, diversifying our revenue streams, and building a strong financial foundation."].

* **Technological Disruption:** Technological disruption can quickly render our products and services obsolete, and we need to stay ahead of the curve. This requires [Suggest specific actions. Examples: "investing in research and development, embracing new technologies, and adapting to changing market conditions."].

Building a Sustainable Future:

Building a sustainable future requires a long-term perspective and a commitment to continuous improvement. This means:

* **Investing in Our People:** Investing in our employees' development and well-being, creating a positive and supportive work environment.
* **Embracing Innovation:** Embracing continuous innovation and adaptation to stay ahead of the competition.
* **Building Strong Relationships:** Building strong relationships with our customers, partners, and investors.

*   **Giving Back to the Community:** Giving back to the community and making a positive impact on the world.

The future of our startup is bright. By staying focused on our long-term vision, embracing continuous innovation, and building a strong and sustainable business, we can achieve our ambitious goals and make a real difference in the world. It's about more than just building a successful company; it's about building a legacy. And that's a journey worth taking. It's about reaching for the stars, not just aiming for them. And with the right vision, the right team, and the right strategy, we can make that dream a reality.

Conclusion

This journey, from a fledgling idea to a scaling enterprise, has been a whirlwind. We've explored the exhilarating highs and the gut-wrenching lows, the strategic planning and the on-the-fly adjustments, the moments of pure inspiration and the grueling hours of hard work. We've learned that building a successful startup isn't just about a brilliant product or a clever business plan; it's about the people, the culture, the relentless pursuit of improvement, and the unwavering belief in your vision.

Remember the early days, fueled by passion and ramen noodles? We've come a long way from those humble beginnings. We've learned to navigate the complexities of funding, the challenges of scaling, and the importance of adapting to a constantly evolving market. We've discovered that success isn't a destination, but a continuous journey of learning, growth, and adaptation.

This book isn't just a guide; it's a testament to the resilience, creativity, and sheer determination required to build something from nothing. It's a celebration of the triumphs and a recognition of the lessons learned along the way. More importantly, it's a roadmap for the future – a blueprint for continued growth, innovation, and impact.

The chapters you've read aren't just theoretical concepts; they're the building blocks of a thriving business. They're the lessons we've learned, the strategies we've implemented, and the challenges we've overcome. They're the foundation upon which we'll continue to build, innovate, and grow.

As you close this book, remember this: the journey of a startup is never truly over. There will always be new challenges, new opportunities, and new lessons to learn. But with the right vision, the right team, and the right mindset, anything is possible. So, go forth, build, innovate, and never stop striving for greatness. The future is yours to shape. Now, go make it happen.